MW00962155

Hey, You...

Get A Life!

The Handbook for the Easily Offended

By Meandria C. Tart-Baskin

Copyright © 2014 by Meandria C. Tart-Baskin

Dedication

This book is dedicated to my mom, Sherry L. Smith-Tart, who was one of the best writers I know. She has written holiday speeches, essays and plays that encouraged the youth at our church, and I will never forget her. I share her passion for the arts and I am grateful to God that her gift lives on through me. Love you mom...to the moon and back...

Love, Mea

TABLE OF CONTENTS

Introduction

*A*wakened from sleep, I felt disgusted from the dream that I had. Although just a dream, the offense seemed very real. In it, one of my closest friends had said that she only pretended to be my friend. She had constantly ducked and dodged me despite my traveling all the way to China to visit her in the hospital. She even kept changing her hospital room! She only revealed this after she accidently ran into me on the elevator. Actually, in real life, this sister in the Lord is actually very sweet. But, I usually take my dreams seriously and try to learn from them. That doesn't mean I'll become paranoid towards my friend because of it. I believe this dream was inspirational because it caused a change in perspective. Something clicked! When it comes to dealing with others, there has to be a balance between thinking both positively and realistically.

As a Christian, I believe that we are all made by God for a specific kingdom purpose. We must not let distractions take us away from our holy directive. Even purpose comes second to sitting at the feet of Christ to learn of Him and become close to Him. We must seek the kingdom of God first and all other things will be added (Matthew 6:33). As we know from the story of Mary and Martha (Luke 10:38-42), both roles that each woman played are important but we must first take time out to spend with our one true and always faithful friend.

There is a song that exclaims "Can't Nobody Do Me like Jesus!" This song rings true because no person will supply every need you have whether emotional, spiritual, or otherwise. That's too much pressure to put on a flawed human being! Every person has a purpose in life. They must find their own destinies. Their function in life is not to make YOU happy. This is not because you are not desirable or special; we all are important to God. That is why we must find our value in Him. Our self-worth must not be based on what others think of us, but solely on what God says we are! *Everyone has their own story. In your life's story, don't make villains and victims, just make yourself a hero. Christ is a hero and we are to be like Christ.*

Those living without a relationship with Christ are searching for that one thing to fulfill them. Everyone does it. They are out for old numero uno, "self". So, whether you are reading this as a Christian or non-Christian, my goal is to let you know: people are not living here just to make YOU happy.

This book is written for everyone: the

IV

person who feels they are the "black sheep" of the family, that wife whose husband barely even looks at her, that mom who's devoted her whole life to her children who rarely call or visit her, the cheating spouse who left his family to be with someone else only to eventually be left alone, the opposite spouse on the other end of the aforementioned topic, the single person who wants to become married, the outcast teenager, the preacher who works hard for others only to find himself underestimated and underappreciated, the worker who doesn't quite fit into the workplace, and last but not least, those who seem to have no friends. Hey, You…Get a Life!

I'm not saying stop doing good works

for others. Just change your attitude about why you do it. No one is going to always give you accolades for what you do. Do it because it makes you a better you. Avoid vilifying those who offend you. We all have our own path to take and each offense can either make or break us. You can surrender to victim mentality, let bitterness fester and become a villain yourself, or you can chose to be a hero.

Jesus is our ultimate example. He loved so many that not only ridiculed him, THEY CRUCIFIED HIM! Although many offenses were piled upon our savior, he never played the victim, was never bitter, and forgave without a second thought. As Christians, we must remember Him and take that attitude "…

Father, forgive them; for they know not what they do"(Luke 23:34). People really don't know what they do. They, like you, are trying to find their own way. Some may stick to a stricter moral code than others, but we are all just trying to find our way. When someone hurts us, they "know not what they do." Most are not deliberately doing anything to us, they are simply trying to find their own way. It doesn't matter how warped their tactics may seem to you, people are generally focused on self. Human beings are flawed, they are hyper-focused on trying to find fulfilment and trying to take care of themselves.

Let's take this journey together. This has been a challenging area for me. As I write and as you read, we are all improving. Each chapter has a hypothetical story with fictional characters and creates solutions for each one of these people. These characters represent real people with real issues of life. If you fit into any of these scenarios, or know of someone who does, you will benefit from this book.

Hopefully these chapters will help you identify and overcome your offenses and put you on the road to living a happy and fulfilling life. You are not alone in your struggle to obtain and maintain joy. Joy is in God and God alone. It can never be found within another human being! I had to learn that by experience. After several years of crying, one day it just clicked! So, whether it's your sibling, parent, child, friend, or spouse… just know that they are only human and will...yeah, I said it…will...hurt you at some point. Some of us wander around trying to find our place like marbles dropped on a flat surface. And like those marbles, someone will bump into us, causing our world to spin out of control. But unlike marbles, we have the ability to control our outcome simply by controlling our response to these tumultuous events.

If you step on somebody knowing that you are hurting them, remember what goes around comes around. Some in the world refer to it as Karma. Whatever you call it, the principle is true. You will reap what you sow, in time. You must "Do unto others as you would have them do unto you" (Luke 6:31 NIV). Never deliberately do something to someone or do something knowing you are going to hurt someone in a major way. Vengeance belongs to the Lord. The only exception to hurting someone's feelings is if God, through his Word, tells you to do or say something that may rub someone the wrong way. You may have to tell someone you are close to the truth about themselves. You will see one of the characters will do this with her relative. God will protect you if you obey his Word.

x

1

Baa, Baa Black Sheep

*M*aybe you feel that you are the odd man out in your family. Maybe it's your immediate family, maybe it's your extended family. Maybe you've heard "you should be more like your sister/brother" so many times it has been imbedded into your being. All is not lost. Just ask our friend Simon.

Simon came from a family of powerful choir singers. He also had some dancers and doctors in his family. Because of the constant self-comparison, he viewed himself as 'Simple Simon' with no real talent, no real spark, unremarkable, and he felt mediocrity looming over his head like a dark cloud. He never did well in school; he tried the church choir, but he was tone deaf and family members told him to give it up. Here he was, in his mid-twenties with no job and no degree. As an escape from the pressure, he began to drink his life away, trying to make himself happy. He would feel a sense of happiness while intoxicated but the hangovers and the reality of his life would all come back to him in the morning. Repeatedly he rehearsed in his head what his mother said, "You should be more like your siblings."

He becomes bitter and he vilifies her and others. "It's her fault" he says. He also blames God for not making him smarter or more talented. He sees his siblings and his cousins' success and it haunts him. He leaves the comfort of his mom's house because he is tired of being reminded of his failure. Now he is homeless. He spends his time going from shelter to shelter or begging for money on street corners. The hurt and pain cuts him deep.

One day, a church group comes to the shelter that he frequents. He hears the Word and cynically listens to it. "Baa," he says. But after the group is done with the sermon, he goes to the outreach coordinator to tell his story. The coordinator, who is also a minister, is lead to give Simon some tough love. The minister knows that although homeless, Simon has a sense of entitlement. He explains to Simon that God loves him and died for his sins and that if God chose to do nothing more than to save him, He has already done enough. He then goes on to tell Simon that the world owes him nothing and lots of others have the same story. "Hey, you…get a life."

The coordinator doesn't stop there, he goes on to ask Simon what his passions are. Simon says that he likes gardening but he expresses to the minister that this isn't an important task and that people don't get recognized for it. He is still comparing his talent to those of his family members. Because he is not a doctor, singer, or dancer, he uses those negative voices in his head to continue the victim's way of thinking. Simon is told the parable about the men and the talents (Matt 25:14-30). Many of you, avid church goers, already know the story. A noble man (God) gave different amounts of talents to three servants. One servant received five, one received two, and the last servant received one. The servant who was given five talents gained five more and the one with two talents gained two more. The last servant with one talent hid his in the ground. The scripture says this servant was full of excuses when the master returned. That unprofitable servant even mentioned fear. But in Simon's case, he was disgusted because he felt his gift was small relative to those around him.

While homeless, Simon stumbled upon a patch of dry and desolate land in the community and began planting fruits and vegetables. Even though Simon had to beg for clothes and money, through the years, he never had to beg for food. He had a natural knack for growing things and was able to grow food for himself throughout this process. He turned that barren space into a community garden. The minister made Simon realize that instead of focusing on his talent, he focused on what others thought of his ability. Remember, his critics are not the villains, Simon had a responsibility to himself to be the hero in his own life's story.

Little did Simon know, this outreach coordinator from the church knew someone who was well off and had some farm land about 30 miles away. This rich gentleman could do nothing with the land and was willing to practically give it away. The coordinator introduced the two of them, and it wasn't long before this farmland began to yield crops from the work of Simon's hands. Elated, the rich man made a deal with Simon. Simon became the owner of the land, while only being obligated to give the rich man 10% of the profits from the fruits and vegetables grown. Many came from miles around for his quality produce. Within a few years' time, Simon built a farmers market and a restaurant from this venture. Today, he's a millionaire.

I shared this story to give an example of how the black sheep's attitude must change. There is not always going to be a magical minister to whisk you away from homelessness. Just have faith in the God who sent the minister. If it doesn't happen the way you think it should, that doesn't mean you are any less worthy than others. Make it happen for you. Get away from victim thinking and live in the here and now. No more fantasy land. No one is going to do it for you. Seek God, find your purpose with God's help and walk in it. "Hey, you…get a life."

2

The Lone Wife

*E*veryone's heard of the lone wolf. This story is about the lone wife - the "woe is me" type of woman whose whole life is to please her husband. When he's away from home, she spends time washing his clothes, cleaning, cooking, buying groceries, and running his errands. She does all this diligently, only to find that when he gets home he barely even speaks to her unless it's to remind her of what bills need to be paid and that she missed a spot while mopping.

She feels angry, alone, and unwanted because she's taken for granted. Look women, I'm not saying don't do these things. I'm saying change your attitude about why you do these things. You do this because you want a clean house, nice healthy food to eat, and money in the bank. You assist him in his endeavors because that's where God has placed you at this time and you do this as unto the Lord. Let him do his own thing. He needs to, because maybe, he's Simon. You know, the guy from the black sheep story. He's finally found his joy.

Let's for the sake of the stories call Simon's wife Launa. Simon had a sad story with tons of issues. He's now a clean-cut millionaire and is living his life. Others stepped on him, but now he's stepping on Launa. Launa is active in the church and so is Simon. It seems that this is the only time the two of them are together. She feels lonely, unloved, and in the back of her mind, she is jealous of her husband's success. She was always on the straight and narrow. Got a degree and now she's at home acting as housekeeper, waitress, cook, and personal assistant.

But one day she decided to embrace her inner hero. She told herself "Hey, you…get a life." She began adding long baths with essential oils, spa days, and web surfing through her days of drudgery. One day while surfing the web, she read an article about a major lawsuit, and an advertisement about going back to school popped up. She always ignored them before, but she had a good feeling about listening to this advertisement. One month after this, she enrolled in law school. Launa finished at the top of her class and broke records with her score on the Bar Exam.

The point here is Launa didn't stop doing household chores. She just scaled back a little to take care of her health and well-being. When she slowed down and enjoyed things that she liked to do and found a new purpose for her tasks, she was able to see her next move. Launa landed a job at the most prestigious law firm in the area, but not immediately after graduation. While waiting on that call, she looked toward heaven. She spent time in prayer and consecration. She asked God how she could enjoy Him more. She thanked God for the sunlight, the smell of roses and the weather.

3

Motherly Love

*W*e all remember Simon's mother, right? Well, by now you're saying, "Who cares about her? Poor Simon should never talk to her again! She's a bad mother." Please don't criticize and vilify Ruthie. Ruthie gave her whole life for her children. She was hard on Simon because she based her own success on how her children turned out. Aaahhh...wrong answer. She's a human being and she made mistakes as all parents do, but the truth is no matter how much we try to pour into our children, free will shapes their destinies. Just ask God, he was the first parent (Gen 3). You can choose Christ and have an abundant life or end up going through life searching for fulfilment in things that are temporary.

Ruthie has seven grown children, six of whom live out of town, including Simon. Even though Simon is doing well and calls her from time to time, they still have a strained relationship. He's working hard each day to forgive her for the many times she compared him to others and hurt his feelings. Of the other five who are out of town, two are doctors, one is a gospel singer, one's a musician and the last child is a ballet dancer. The one in town is Sarah, who is also a doctor. Sarah is a cosmetic surgeon who has a very successful practice. Outside of work, she attends benefit dinners, and is active in her church.

Ruthie is a church mother at a different church from her children and all of the members show appreciation for her. (She gets all types of appreciation from her fellow church members, but still longs for that from her children) However, she only hears from her children once a week on alternate days. She remembers how she worked two jobs at one point to start a college fund for the children and she's heard "thank you" but she doesn't see the children's actions match this. When she needs something like a trip to the market or someone to eat dinner with, she calls on Sarah. But when she calls, Sarah's often working, at a benefit dinner, or in church. Sarah has one day she dedicates to Ruthie and she makes sure that one day is always cleared.

When her children are unhappy about something, Ruthie worries. Worry can take its toll on the body. Ruthie has suffered several strokes and is very blessed to still be able to walk. She is still weak on her right side and has been unable to drive at all or walk very far without her cane or walker. Ruthie often feels sad and lonely, but instead of letting it go into victimhood, she reaches for God. He is her comforter. One day, through prayer and tears, she is lead to do seven days of prayer and consecration.

She wakes up at 5am each morning, worships and reads her Bible, prays again at noon to break her fast and prays right before bed. At the end of her 7 days of consecration, she sat down to watch some television, and the minute she turns it on, she saw a commercial. This commercial advertises a device developed by a physical therapist to bring strength to certain limbs of the body. She's a little skeptical, but orders it anyway. It's supposed to come within two weeks. While she is waiting, she goes back into her consecration.

Ruthie goes outside and takes a short walk with her cane around the corner and ends up in a nearby pet shop. She falls in love with a black Labrador Retriever puppy and takes him home. She names him Sam.

She's so busy taking care of Sam that she forgets about the device she ordered. When it arrives, she starts using it right away. Even though it doesn't work instantly, the results are gradual and that is good enough for her! She doesn't get frustrated or give up. By that next year, she has full use of her right side and she walks Sam every day.

Mother Ruthie got a life! Since then, she's cancelled or rescheduled at least one date with Sarah a month as well as missed at least one of her children's calls because she's gone to the Puppy and me spa with

Sam. She started a monthly fellowship with the other seniors in her church and her children smile when they talk about her joy. A lot of the church youth attend the monthly seniors' fellowship and ask her about life and how to overcome obstacles. She responds "Hey, you…get a life" and keeps on going.

In her offense state, this mother worried, was sad, and was unfulfilled. When she began to focus upward (on God) and inward (self), she found happiness. She became reacquainted with her own interests and passions and learned to "get a life" outside of others.

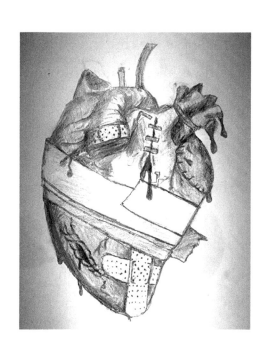

4

Your Cheating Heart

Sarah was married when she first started her practice. She was married to a guy named Blake. Blake was similar to Simon, in that he was average high school and not musically talented. However, he seemed to have high self-esteem because a lot of girls found him physically attractive. He was a high school athlete, but he was best at body building. As he grew older, he realized that a lot of women he was interested in steered clear of him as "the gorgeous man" and they preferred the successful, "average looking" guys. He had always been told "You're as dumb as a stump, but you are so hot." He was treated like the stereotypical dumb blonde. But this was far from who he actually was. Because people focused on how attractive he was, they did not know that he attended college with Sarah on a sports scholarship and applied himself academically while there.

When he went on dates, women would just look at his lips instead of listening to what came out of them. He was very intelligent, articulate, and funny, but others didn't notice. They just noticed his physique. Sarah seemed to be the only person that was into Blake, the whole person. It was because of this that Blake was drawn to her. Upon graduation, he made Sarah his wife.

Sarah finished medical school and Blake pursued a career in investment banking with his finance degree. When the economy tanked, Blake lost his job and was out of work for three years. However, Sarah's career was thriving. Blake was fine with being out of work since their only debt at that point was Sarah's school loans.

One night, he attended a big benefit dinner with her as he always did in support of her. This night, Sarah told a joke around her fellow doctors about him being her "trophy husband." Upset and embarrassed, he found an excuse to leave the dinner early.

Furious from the offense that night, he went to talk to their mutual friend, Lisa. Lisa was a friend who went to college with the two of them. She was the pretty, bubbly, cheerleader type that every girl wanted to look like. She was a freshman when they were juniors. Lisa dropped out after her mother passed away. Lisa's mother had left her an inheritance and a huge insurance policy. Blake showed her an investment that had her set for life. Because of this, to Lisa, he was the smartest man on earth. Lisa never married because she just hadn't "found the right guy."

Lisa listened to Blake rant the night of the "trophy husband" incident and set a future date for him to come over for coffee instead of attending Sarah's next event.

After several trips to Lisa's, while Sarah was left to attend her benefit dinners alone, Blake felt he was in love with Lisa. One thing lead to another and Lisa said she was pregnant with Blake's baby. Excited about the baby, Blake told Sarah about the affair and pushed for a divorce.

Lisa told Blake that she loved him during this period of time, but this was far from true. When the divorce was final, Blake returned to Lisa's only to find that there was another man there and the baby was not his.

Devastated, he climbed into a bottle like his ex brother-in law Simon did. Drunken and dirty, he crawled back to Sarah to ask for a second chance. Sarah accepted her responsibility in the matter, but said, "NO!. Hey, you…get a life!" He had nowhere to go but his cousin's house. Her name was Brenda. Brenda let him stay there and he spent two more months feeling sorry for himself.

This cousin of his was a praise and worship leader who had been single all of her adult life. She was very happy and constantly prayed for Blake who just couldn't seem to get it together after being betrayed by Lisa. He mentioned the last words that his ex-wife said to him and Brenda told him that Sarah was right.

Although this hurt his feelings, Brenda had to tell her cousin the truth.

Brenda told him to really think about how Sarah felt during the divorce process. Sure, she seemed fine the last day he saw her, but she suffered a lot because of Blake. Sarah was making a lot of money and supported him while he was out of work and now she was still doing it in the divorce. Every time she wrote that alimony check, she probably cringed because it was not fair to support someone who hurt her so badly.

Blake talked with Brenda more throughout the night. He cried as he began to see things from Sarah's side of the story. He even began to forgive Lisa. Lisa didn't know what she was doing. She didn't subscribe to a strict moral code and he knew that. She didn't know any better. She was just doing her own thing, finding purpose in all the wrong places. Lisa did not deliberately hurt Blake, she just valued her own feelings with no consideration for how it affected others

Blake asked God for forgiveness. He chose to leave his feelings of offense behind. He was no longer the victim. He began to go to church with Brenda. He realized that he could play the drums. He got better and better at it. He began to apply for several banking jobs, but none seemed to call back.

One of the church members was the CEO of a new financial services company. Brenda slipped him Blake's resume. He got a call for an interview and finally an offer! With the base pay plus commissions, he was making the six-figure income he always wanted. He went to court to stop the alimony. He brought with him flowers and candy to give to Sarah. He knew Sarah didn't owe him anything. She didn't have to ever take him back. He did this out of the kindness of his heart and expected nothing in return. Several years later, they remarried.

Blake's story is a classic case of how people sometimes let their own insecurities cause them to hurt others. We have all heard the saying "hurt people, hurt people." This story is a prime example of that. Instead of communicating with his wife, he played the victim, and went outside of his marriage for comfort.

While in a marital relationship, before taking any drastic action, stop to verbalize to your spouse that something was done or said to offend you. Blake was so angry, he wanted to hurt Sarah, but what he was actually doing was giving away his power to both Sarah and Lisa instead of looking to God for healing from his mental anguish.

5

A Woman Scorned

So, you know where I am going with this, right? Yes, I know you are ready to hear Sarah's side of the story. Sarah was not gullible and after Blake missed the fourth benefit dinner, he began to get a little sloppy. With each visit to Lisa, he began to care less and less if he got caught. Lisa had time to feed his ego, making him feel special the way she did with all of the guys. Blake's actions left Sarah feeling insecure, unloved, and unattractive.

Sarah always viewed herself as a plain Jane. She was not really tall, not really short, and not voluptuous. To her, she was just ok in the looks department. All women have things that they don't like about their looks, Sarah had at least ten and took comfort in the fact that she always knew she was smart. But that wasn't enough for her. She tried to become the epitome of perfection, choosing cosmetic surgery as her field of expertise. She had colleagues perform ten procedures on her without telling anyone she had anything done. People noticed that she looked good, but no one noticed how drastic the changes were.

After the cheating was confirmed and

before Blake actually pushed for divorce, she started going in for more and more Botox treatments. The night he asked for a divorce, Sarah cried all night. As soon as she could, she got breast implants. She thought if she made herself look better than Lisa, she would feel better about the divorce. She did for a while, but these outward changes attracted too much of the wrong attention in the dating scene. Several painful rebounds later, she put on a façade and went to another benefit dinner.

While mingling at the dinner, a male server smiled at her and told her to meet him outside in front of the building for a talk. There was something special about this young man, so she agreed. He told her that God told him that she was suffering. He even told her everything that she had been going through. She cried, because she knew that this random man did not travel in the same circles she did, so how could he know? He reached into his pocket and pulled out a small Bible. He offered to give her the number to the church's prayer line. In the front of the bible, where the name belongs, he wrote the number and underneath he wrote "Hey, you...get a life." They chuckled and then he offered to pray for her on the spot. She agreed to the prayer and felt better after that.

Sarah called that prayer line the next day. She decided to devote what little free time she had left to getting closer to God. She set aside a time to visit her mom and became active in her church. She looked around for the mysterious server because she wanted to say thank you. He was nowhere to be found. She didn't even see him at the next benefit dinner she attended. And when she asked about him, no one knew who she was talking about. Was he an angel?

No, his name was Minister Washington. He belonged to a different church and had given Sarah the prayer line number to an affiliate church closer to where she lived. He was only at the dinner volunteering his services for just that week.

Sarah didn't dwell on the absence of the mysterious stranger. She just smiled about the valuable information given to her. Sarah knew her focus needed to be on God and improving her "person." She started doing free surgeries for low income children with burn injuries. As she worked, she didn't look over her shoulder for some guy to whisk her off her feet. She was enjoying every bit of her life and service to others.

She began to see her own struggle. She even saw things from Blake's point of view. She realized he was a flawed human being that craved validation. She realized that she is more than her beauty and although it was natural for her to want to adorn herself, she needed to realize she had a purpose. She needed to find God's purpose for her life and cultivate that passion inside of her instead of fantasizing about how to get back at Blake. Blake had his own issues to deal with. It was time to think about her own mission. By her concentrating on her purpose, God allowed her and Blake to remarry several years later.

Two halves cannot create a whole. Sometimes we need restoration and redirection when life seems to throw us unexpected circumstances. This time of separation allowed Sarah to become reacquainted with herself and find purpose outside of her husband. Once again, she put the power in her own hands to put happiness in her grasp. She didn't embrace victim mentality, she didn't wallow in bitterness and become a villain, she became the hero of her own story.

6

Every Single Day

*B*lake's cousin Brenda, as said before, had been single all her adult life. Her parents raised her in the church and she had always been a "good" girl. Now forty years old, she had some challenges in being single. She had been hurt by several guys because of her stance on romance. She would not settle for less, because she knew that she needed someone that shared her religious beliefs.

She loved too deeply in the past and got extremely hurt. One guy seemed like he loved her, but kept breaking up with her to hook up with other girls because he could not practice abstinence until marriage. Brenda thought this was because the other girls were more attractive than her, but in reality, this guy was just another selfish person, doing his own thing. He felt like he needed sex to find his joy, and he wasn't doing it with Brenda, so he eventually broke it off one last time for good.

Some people hurt us in the process of finding themselves. We become pawns in their little game to fuel their ego. Fulfillment can never be found in an attachment to another person! Some people constantly hurt others because they may have been hurt before or something inside them feels empty. They leave a trail of broken hearts along the way. But for what reason? They have none. They simply move on and devour the next person like a black hole. Person after person is used and abused. They drain the life force from everyone they come in contact with.

They manipulate, they con, and they are never happy. They use and throw people away like used tissues. They have not gotten the message. It is them, not you that needs to get a life.

Brenda moved on to another guy. He was a member of her church. He, too, was a bit of a playboy. He stated he was too young to be tied down and needed to find himself. He went into the military and wrote Brenda from time to time, but after a few years, the letters dwindled and she finally got a call from him. He was calling to say he was getting married to someone else! Brenda was devastated. Why was this happening to her? Was it her? No…It just wasn't her time yet. But when was her time?

She was angry, but she did not become angry with God. She kept serving and witnessing to others. She kept writing songs for the praise and worship team. Every time she would get a negative thought concerning those who hurt her, she would get on her knees to pray. She chose not to wallow in her offense and chose not to become the victim. Brenda was also having a lot of trouble at work with her supervisor, Kristi. Kristi, a former praise and worship leader herself, was always nitpicking Brenda's work. We will later learn that Kristi went through church hurt and took that out on someone representing the institution that hurt her. Kristi, though quite annoying, was harmless. She just added to Brenda's internal stressors.

Brenda began saving her money for things she was passionate about. She dipped into her savings once a month for things like monthly makeovers, spa days and trips to the movies on her own. She melted down a promise ring that one of her significant others once gave her. She had it formed into a ring that spelled out "JESUS." She wore that on her ring finger where an engagement ring would have been.

After much saving, she finally had enough money to go into the studio. Brenda and the worship team from her church recorded a few of her songs. The engineer was very busy so it took quite some time before it was ready for release. But Brenda didn't panic. She just enjoyed herself while in the studio. She carried on like this for five more years. She was patient and steadfast, not letting time make a victim out of her. Within that five years, her cousin Blake came to live with her. Her CD was complete and ready for the mix and master. A year after that, about the same time Blake got on his feet, it was finally released.

Four more years after that, she got signed with an up and coming record label in Chicago. The owner's name was Adam. Brenda and Adam really hit it off. Brenda was now fifty years old. Adam was also in his fifties. He never married because he was too busy chasing his dreams. After one dream would fail, he would jump to another. He was enjoying life too much to settle down and get married. He did his dirt in the past and broke a lot of hearts; in the same process, he also got his heart broken. They exchanged stories and laughed at how sensitive they once were.

One day, as Adam met Brenda for lunch, he talked even more about the mistakes of his past. He looked at her and she looked at him. "Hey, you…get a life," they said to each other. Adam proposed to Brenda, now fifty-two, and they had a happy life together. They enjoyed 25 years of marriage before Brenda went to meet the Lord with a smile on her face.

It is important for us not to be impatient with the Lord's timing. They enjoyed a rich life as married seniors, but Brenda had a rich life before Adam and the record deal. She enjoyed her home church, treating herself to dinners and a movie, and she enjoyed encouraging others, like her cousin Blake.

It is also important for us to remember

that once we get what we want, if in fact
what we want is in God's will, we don't
lose sight of its place. Those desires are
only secondary to our relationship with
Christ. In the case with Brenda and
Adam, the two of them were in love, but
they weren't so attached to each other
that Adam would give up living after
Brenda's death. He knew that she had
finished her course and he was looking to
do the same. When it comes to the things
of God, it is an individual affair. When in
his late seventies, Adam sold his record
company to become a motivational
speaker for troubled youth in the area. He
is still doing it today.

At 85 years old, he wears the title of
evangelist. He travels every week to

different youth services, while spending every Sunday morning at his home church, gleaning from his pastor.

As a single, learn to enjoy your life. Thank God for every day. Remember, singles have the advantage according to the Bible (1 Corinthians 7:32-40). Your focus is on God and God alone and you don't have the added task of trying to juggle a spouse in your daily routine.

Marriage can be very difficult to juggle. Spend too little time with that spouse and you damage the relationship. Spend too much time and you lose yourself only to find that that spouse doesn't appreciate the sacrifices that you have made. You are blessed. And every single day must be enjoyed and lived to the fullest. Use the Word of God as your gauge to avoid sin and have a Holy Ghost party!

7

Why Outcast, Oh My Soul?

This is the story of Lisa, who disrupted the life of Blake and many of the men she came in contact with. You see, Blake didn't know the details of Lisa's past. Sure, he knew that Lisa's mom was a single mother, but nothing more. The story of Lisa's mom was nothing abnormal. Much like countless others, Lisa's mom fell hard for someone who wasn't for her and did so at a young age.

After having Lisa, she worked hard to provide for her only child. She worked her way up at a car manufacturing plant and lived very modestly. Lisa didn't know this at the time, but her mother had saved up quite a bit of money and also had purchased a large life insurance policy.

Because her mom was always working, Lisa was often alone. So she was more vulnerable to victimhood when offenses came. She was not taught hero mentality. When younger, she was left in daycare, but as she became a preteen, it was decided that she could get a key to the house. Lisa began to seek the attention of young men at school. These boys and other girls at school treated Lisa like she was invisible. Lisa would come home every day crying. One day some girls on the bus put gum in her hair. All the children laughed at her as she ran away crying.

Lisa felt unattractive and unloved. She found other so called "outcasts" and started her own clique. This made her feel better, even though Lisa's circle of friends were being terrorized by a group of bully girls at school, that caused them emotional distress. This support group of friends helped Lisa until one day it all came to a screeching halt. One of the bully girls was editor of the school newspaper and published a column entitled "the fashion police." In it, she bashed the clothing and style of one of the girls in Lisa's clique and offered suggestions on how this girl could change her style.

The little girl took it so hard, that she took several pain pills and committed suicide. The bully received no punishment. The only thing done was the school banned the column from the school newspaper and forced the writer to resign as editor.

The ring leader's name was Wendy. Seeing Wendy and her clique parade around the school like nothing happened caused Lisa and her clique to go to the school administration to see if her friend could be avenged somehow. When she went to the school administrators, they said there was nothing they could do. The school system totally failed her! No one there pointed her in the direction of true help. The friendships of Lisa's clique became strained over time and eventually dissipated. Can you guess who was a part of Wendy's clique? Sarah, the plastic surgeon, Blake's wife, of course.

With her group of friends disbanded, Lisa was out for blood. In her offense, she was not equipped with the mental fortitude to embrace the hero mentality so she fell prey to victimhood and became a villain. She sought out how she could get revenge. She went to the library to do some research. After reading several law books, she found that there was nothing legally she could do about the situation, since it there were no laws at the time that offered justice for her friend.

She looked at the article that she

believed "killed" her friend. She began to research on how to make herself beautiful. She had a dirty plot cooking and wasn't afraid to put it into action. She was now heading into her junior year in high school.

She got a job at the local fast food restaurant for extra money. (Note: her mom was extremely frugal and worried about the future, so she was not aware of mom's savings). When her mom asked why she wanted the job, Lisa didn't tell her the big plan. So, mom assumed that she was just sad about her friend and needed an outlet to cope with her grief.

Lisa bought a new outfit every pay period. She also got hair extensions and false lashes, put on acrylic nails, and got her eyebrows arched with every other paycheck. She felt good, looked good, and other teens began to take notice. Remember her library trip? She put the law books down and researched the psychology of attraction. She knew ways to attract boys that other girls would often sit and dream of. She studied techniques tailored to each personality type. She was ready for revenge.

That year in high school, she stole every boyfriend that Wendy had. Into adulthood, the rest is history. She was highly motivated to execute vengeance on the group of people that caused her pain. She slept with every woman's husband that was in that clique. Her plan was complete when she attracted the attention of Sarah's husband. She thought very little of men and other women. She was a robot driven by revenge and revenge alone. Until… she had her daughter, Ariel.

At the root of it all, Lisa was still hurting inside well into her adulthood. But when her child came into the world, she had a new responsibility. It has to be recognized that this child was not born to end her suffering, no. However, she knew she had to get it together because she didn't want Ariel to live the life she did. She wanted a life of joy for her child. She prayed to God and came to Christ.

She is now full of the Spirit and no longer feels that pain. She thought revenge would fill that void, but it didn't make her feel any better. Vengeance is mine; I will repay, saith the Lord (Romans 12:19). She has then written letters of apology to all the wives she's hurt. Many of them have forgiven her.

Not every story is wrapped in a neat little bow. Lisa's story took a long time to unfold. The hurt, grief, and trauma caused her to behave in this manner. She had to let go of the grief and unforgiveness to free herself. She may seem like a villain, but she was once a victim. And she had to learn to be the hero in her own story. She had to save herself by surrendering to Christ.

8

Don't Be Weary in Well Doing

*W*e all remember the preacher from the homeless shelter who ministered to Simon, our black sheep. His name was Elder John. He was promoted to Outreach Coordinator of the church at that time, but it wasn't always this way. Coming off the streets as an ex-gang affiliate, he was on fire for God. One day as he was in the park passing drugs, he heard singing. John was intrigued. He followed the singing to a tent and there he found a group of older ladies singing gospel music. He didn't grow up listening to this and liked the sound of something different. After the concert, there was an altar call. John went right up for prayer and felt the Holy Spirit for the first time. He was afraid, but since that day, he never looked back.

Everyone enjoyed his testimony. He was always there for anyone who needed him. He would go to the homes of the elderly once a week and go door to door witnessing on his own. He brought five different visitors to church every Sunday. As a result, there were 50 new members joining every year. This was documented by Pastor Brown because John hadn't kept count.

One day it became time for the church to elect and Outreach Coordinator. John applied for the position because it was a passion of his. Besides, he was already doing the job of Outreach Coordinator on his own. There were two other candidates for the position: one church mother who had been a member of the church for twenty years but had never done outreach before and a new member who was Outreach Coordinator for ten years at another church out of town.

The new member, Brian, came from Dayton, Ohio. He was invited by Elder John to come to church one Sunday just last year. Needless to say, Brian was elected. Elder John was devastated. He was angry, but still did his work for the

Lord. He prayed every time he felt the anger rise up and even talked to the pastor about how he felt. The pastor prayed with him and by the following year, Elder John was no longer angry about the decision. He picked up more outreach tasks and worked closely with Brian to accomplish membership goals. He followed up on the members that hadn't returned and added local homeless shelters to the effort.

By the following year, it was election time again. Elder John didn't even run! So, the mother got the position. He worked closely with her and Brian was now the Assistant Coordinator. John delegated duties like a pro and the outreach team was just the faithful three. They created subcommittees to handle different ministries: the homeless, the prison, the elderly, and the streets. Their team of three grew to fifteen faithful workers. The next year rolled around and no one applied for the Outreach Coordinator position. The pastor then decided to appoint Elder John and he has been in that position ever since.

And whatsoever ye do, do it heartily, as to the Lord, and not unto men; Knowing that of the Lord, ye shall receive the reward of the inheritance: for ye serve the Lord Christ (Colossians 3:23-24).

Some people never get recognized or rewarded for their diligence in working for Christ. However, it is our faith in God and love for Him that should energize and motivate us to keep working. We work

69

because we love God. We work because we believe in our mission to spread the Gospel.

9

Not a Good 'Fit' For the Company

*W*e all remember Minister Washington, the server, from Sarah's story. Minister Washington showed her love and told her to "get a life." This was exactly what Minister Washington was doing. He was highly educated, with a Doctor of Divinity and an MBA. Minister Washington worked for a local packaging firm in an office environment. While 95% of the employees of the packaging firm worked in the warehouse segment of the company and wore "comfortable" clothing, Minister Washington dressed business professional. He also used correct grammar when speaking and didn't use foul language at all. These differences caused him to not quite hit it off with his coworkers.

During lunches and breaks, the workers would always laugh and talk, but as soon as Minister Washington walked into the room, they would get quiet. Nothing was wrong with the minster, but despite the fact that he was well dressed at all times and came off very confident, he really wasn't. He wanted so bad to be a success at work that it was all he thought about. He would often daydream about becoming Senior Vice President. His performance on the job was stellar. He provided detailed reports, excellent presentations, and received near perfect quarterly evaluations. But after seven years, he was still in the same role. To add insult to injury, none of his coworkers even talked to him.

After several more months, the packaging company met the fate that so many companies face today. The company was sold and the new owners decided to make some cutbacks. They did away with several positions within the company including Minister Washington's. He was left without a job but was given a generous severance package. He prayed to God about his next move. Confused, he clung closer to God and began a scheduled prayer routine. He strengthened his relationship with the Lord and began to do random volunteer work. The Lord told him which places to seek out day by day.

This is where he met Sarah. Because of his job loss, Minister Washington was at the right place at the right time to minister to someone having a hard time.

That next week was his week to volunteer at the nursing home. He mopped the floors, cleaned the rooms, and spent time with lonely residents that rarely got visitors. He spent a month volunteering there and God told him to move on to the next ministry. Minister Washington got a permit for a street corner. Dressed well, but casual, he had a microphone, and he sang and preached for the Lord. A guy in a Mercedes Benz stopped in the lot to ask for prayer. He had just finished visiting his sister at a nearby hospital and she wasn't doing too well. Minister Washington prayed for him right at that moment and was lead to leave his post to go pray for the man's sister at the hospital. There was no immediate manifestation, but the two men believed God. That following week, the sister was showing improvements. By the end of that month, she was completely healed!

Minister Washington and this gentleman became close friends. This man, whose name was Don, revealed that he was CEO of a popular Christian radio station. There was tremendous support all over the city and it was well-funded. Minister Washington revealed to his new friend his educational background. He now works directly under Don at the radio station and is sometimes called upon to be a radio personality. Minister Washington finally received the title Senior Vice President and felt successful enough to recognize himself as Dr. Washington.

In this story, our character finds comfort in serving God. When you are not a good fit for the world around you, don't get discouraged. As a Christian, we are to be in the world but not of the world. We must learn to celebrate our difference from the world around us. God made us all unique.

We are all a part of the body of Christ and we all have our functions. If we compare our functions to the natural body, each part is important. We all think about the ear, the head, and the feet. But I sometimes think of the unseen organs, like the kidneys, liver, and heart. Although these organs cannot be seen, they are very vital to the functioning of the body. What people do behind the scenes to move the work of God forward is just as important as these vital organs. Intercessors are like those vital internal organs that are the glue to a functioning body.

10

To BFF or Not to BFF

Do you remember Brenda's supervisor, Kristi, who gave Brenda trouble on many occasions at work? She was annoying because of what she had gone through in her life. You see, Kristi was a woman with no friends. Every time someone tried to get close to Kristi she pulled away. She's been hurt before by so-called friends.

Kristi had a pretty decent childhood

and had several close friends. She was very athletic and popular and did well in school. Everything seemed well for Kristi until she realized that she was not like the other girls. You see, Kristi had homosexual tendencies that had not become apparent to her until her teen years. She experimented with this well into her college years, but came to know Christ during her last year of college. She was determined to put this lifestyle behind her and though challenging, she had some success.

She denied every urge she had daily, devoting most of her life to prayer, fasting, and reading the Bible. She became active in all of the campus Christian ministries and things were looking up for her. Kristi got to the point where her urges were no more. She was too focused on the future and God's purpose to think about anything else.

Before we finish her story, let me digress. This story is controversial in the fact that hardly anyone believes that these urges can be stopped. Also, there may be some bashers out there that believe that God hates the homosexual. Well I've got some news for them. God loves us all, but he hates all sin. Those who are not ready for Him will not be able to go with Him when He comes. It's a daily fight for all of us, but we must do all we can to be faultless when He comes. We're ready when we can consistently sing "I've been saved all day, no evil have I done!"

All unrighteousness is sin (I John 5:17). So, adultery and fornication can be grouped with Kristi's sin. We all know people who were able to abstain from sinful behavior despite the constant pull of the flesh to act outside of God's will. We know single people who have kept themselves for several years and we know several married people who were faithful to each other for years. Because these shining examples exist, all things are possible! We are not defined by our sin. Our impure urges may try to creep back in at times, but we can all fight our respective vices with the Word of God. It's a daily fight, but it is attainable.

While serving God to the fullest, Kristi gets her first real trial. A new girl named

Dinah joins the church and Dinah seems really nice. However, she's a wolf in sheep's clothing. Dinah secretly wants to replace Kristi as the church's choir director. She will do anything to get that position.

Dinah gradually gets closer to Kristi. So close in fact, that they share testimonies. Kristi tells Dinah about her past. This is something that Kristi never stated in front of the congregation. Dinah seems to treat Kristi with respect despite this new information. Kristi goes on to serve the Lord with no problem. One day, she goes to choir rehearsal and all the choir members are already there talking. The talking is indistinct and the choir stops chatting when she enters the room.

Dinah is standing in the front of the choir. Dinah informed Kristi that she had been voted out of the choir. Some of the women chuckled and one woman clutched her baby. Kristi walks out with her head hung low and the choir resumes talking with no regard to her feelings.

When she goes to work the next day, she takes the whole incident out on her subordinates. Brenda, who she knows does praise and worship, gets the worst of it. No one on the job knows what's going on. They just know that Kristi is extra snippy and snarky about the quality of their work.

Kristi tells her pastor about the whole story with Dinah. He openly rebukes the choir members because he knows that

Kristi is living a good life. Despite the support of her pastor, she is still too embarrassed to come back to church. The pastor prays with her and recommends another church to her that one of his friends pastors. When Kristi attends the new church, she tells the new pastor everything. The new pastor recommends that she meet with one of the elders of his church.

When she has the meeting with elder, Elder Black, she finds that he too shared her struggle with homosexuality. The two of them get to know each other and become very good friends.

Then, something unique happened as they work for the Lord together. They realize they make a good team.

One year later, Elder Black proposed to Kristi. She now found a suitable BFF. They now have five children and she still works at the company where Brenda once served under her.

Again, someone finds themselves offended by someone they trusted. Kristi projected this hurt onto her subordinates at work until she looked upward and inward. Once God became the focus in her life, she was able to find happiness and a thriving relationship put together by God. Struggles have not totally gone away, but surrendering to God was the first step.

Everyone battles ungodly urges and it is a daily fight to remain in right standing with God. Just as the homosexual may struggle with his or her urges, the heterosexual may be tempted with infidelity if they are married, and fornication if they are single. When you live a life devoted to God and His ways, He will take care of you, keep you, strengthen you, and settle you.

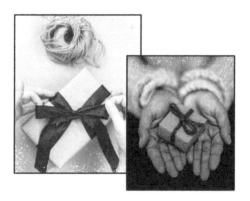

11

Tying it All Together

*W*hether you are a Kristi, a Simon, a Launa, a Lisa, a Blake, a Brenda, or any other character displayed here, you can get a life. The concepts here seem very simple, but these stories make the concept come alive. It did that for me and I hope that it will do the same for you. In each scenario, there were two main themes: God and purpose. A person will do well in life if she or he realizes that these are most important in life. We are created with a God sized hole in our hearts and to fill it, we must serve the purpose He gives us.

Purpose to me reminds me of seeing a cluster of ants on the ground. They would usually clutter towards something sweet that maybe a child left on the ground. The tasty treat is too big for just one ant to carry, so each ant is responsible for carrying his piece. Human beings sometimes can be really cruel when this process is taking place. Instead of watching the wonder of nature, they sometimes become grossed out and begin to eliminate the ants through extermination or by simply stepping on them. Sometimes a few of the ants are able to get through.

Satan our enemy, like a human with the ants, is disgusted by the very sight of us. He seeks to steal, kill, and destroy. But we have no reason to fear. We just need to know that we have an appointed time to work the work that God has assigned for us and we need not delay. The sweet morsel is our purpose in life, dropped down in our hearts by God above. The treat is big enough for all of us to have a piece and we must each carry our own to the hill. Instead of wasting valuable time looking at others, we need to focus on our God and our piece of purpose.

12

Thinking Positively,
but Realistically

*W*hile writing this book, I received my wake-up call. In the past, I couldn't receive constructive criticism from loved ones because I thought they were just putting me down. But you, the reader, can take criticism from me because I don't know you. I don't know how you look, act, or the thoughts in your head, so the following comments are not an attack on your personal being. These are statements I had to say to myself first, before writing them to encourage and inspire you.

While fighting to maintain a positive and realistic attitude in dealings with others, there are five actions available to help you achieve this: Conquering Clinginess, Ditch the Daydreaming, Jilt Being Judgmental, Erase Emotions, and Guard Your Gates. The characters in this book all had to do this to "get a life." They had to focus on God first, and second, their own purpose in serving Him.

Conquering Clinginess

 The scripture says you are to love your neighbor as you love yourself (Mark 12:31), but if somewhere deep inside, you don't love yourself, how can you really love others? Sure, it's fine to serve others, but do so as unto the Lord not even looking too closely at them.

We are not to expect anything from anyone or any institution. Too many people I see, myself included, complain because they have a never-ending sense of entitlement. They think the whole world owes them something. Momma doesn't owe you a thing because she said something you do not like. Your kids don't owe you anything, they did not ask to be born. Your spouse owes you nothing because you said, "I do." Neither does that job, the government, nor your colleagues because of your education. Your course is charted by God and God alone and nothing is by accident. So, get the chip off your shoulder!

I once had a dream that I was in front of God in judgment. The Lord told me that I placed my self-esteem into all of my accomplishments and not on Him. I remember weeping and being surprised that this was God's response. I had always thought that I gave Him glory for everything I had accomplished. Ever since then, I've tried to understand what He was saying to me. Now I do! I get it,

Lord. I was blind to the fact that I was thirsty for accolades and always fishing for compliments. Playing the victim, I did not realize that I was seeking validation outside of Christ. I worked really hard at everything I did and when my efforts went unnoticed by those around me or I was criticized despite how hard I worked, I fell deeper into depression.

This is how clinginess can harm your wellbeing. Nothing can be gained by being dependent on others to make you happy. It can cause anger and bitterness because you become angry at those who seem to underestimate you or who don't get excited about your vision.

Remember the story of Joseph and how his brothers and even his father felt about his vision (Genesis 37)? Joseph had a dream that the sun, the moon and the eleven stars bowed to him. To those of you who don't know the story, this implied that Joseph's mother, father, and eleven brothers were going to be subordinate to him. It was a dream that eventually came true, but he was hated by his brothers for telling it.

Why would anyone who heard something like that jump on board and celebrate? Joseph's brothers could have been able to celebrate if they "got a life." Instead of judging Joseph and hating him, they could have sought God for their own visions and been content in those subservient roles. But that's not how the story went. However, we learn several dynamics in this story. Dynamics about vision, dynamics about forgiveness, and dynamics about acceptance. Joseph had to go through servitude and struggle before his vision came to pass. He also had to forgive those who seemed to be responsible for his struggle. He really could have thanked his brothers, because they played a role in his current elevation.

Others are still trying to find their own way. They don't have time to stroke your ego. Not even the ones that are supposed to "love" you or be "in love" with you. Expect nothing from anyone except God and don't try to figure out when or what to expect. Enjoy the here and now. If you expect nothing, anything that comes will be a pleasant surprise. Learn to be grateful for the little things. Be grateful for the breath of life God puts into you each morning, because it could very well stop. Our goal is to be ready for that great day.

This brings us to our next concept: Ditch the Daydreaming. Gone are the days for you that involve you sitting on your cot thinking about your win of a million dollars and being disappointed when you don't win the sweepstakes. Go out and make your million one dollar at a time! You may feel that people are against you. This is not the case. They're barely even thinking of you because they have their own purpose to fulfil. If you want it, get it. Pray and God will answer. There is a quote from a song that says "If the gas runs out my car…I'll just walk because it's in my heart." No one's going to give you anything. Believe enough in yourself to invest in yourself.

Dreaming big is perfectly ok. I am all for that. However, calling things that be not as though they were (Romans 4:17) doesn't mean you can have everything you want, when you want. Approach your desires with this attitude: If He doesn't deliver us, we know He's able (Daniel 3:17-18). This may sound like a church cliché, but it's really not. God is so far above us. He knows what's best for us and what things will turn us away from Him. We were created to praise and worship the Lord and serve Him. This is why not everyone will be rich, not everyone will be married, and not everyone will be famous. God knows what will turn us away from Him. It is not because we were any less intelligent, desirable, or talented that we didn't achieve it. It is just not our piece of sweet destiny.

Jilt Being Judgemental

 This next concept neatly ties into the Conquering Clinginess concept. You know the type: "Ooo girl, did you see

what she had on?" or "That waitress doesn't know what she is doing." Some judgmental people may have been hurt before by extreme dependency on another person and use judgement as a coping mechanism. Maybe they have depended on their spouse for attention and snubbed the sister in the short dress because they think their husband is looking at her. Maybe the rude customer at the restaurant got passed over for a promotion and felt the need to point out his waitress' incompetency.

Even though there are Christians out there who have committed sins and had to repent, there are some out there that have remained "unspotted from the world". Some Christians may feel that a strict lifestyle is all they have going for them. Because of this insecurity, they find themselves engaging in gossip and putting others down to make themselves feel better. In that, they are no better than the brother or sister who engaged in the sinful act. They talk about their brother's past failures long after he's been reclaimed. God is not pleased with this. If you are one that steps on the others, that diverts you from your purpose. This is not how heroes act.

Erase Emotions

 I find all of these a challenge, but this, by far is the most challenging. It

ties into the next concept I will mention: Guarding Your Gates, which I will address in more detail later. This is a neat little saying, but I'm not expecting myself, or anyone, to completely erase their emotions. We are humans with emotions and it is emotions that make us more alive as caregivers, workers, and singers. However, we can erase emotions from our decisions. There are many instances when emotions can take you out of the will of God.

Blake was a prime example. He let the comment about being a "trophy husband" drive him out of his marriage. In a more common occurrence, anger could rise and make you say or do something you really shouldn't say or do.

A guy at the restaurant demeaned his waitress because he had a bad day at work. He didn't get loud and use bad language, but he did make her feel incompetent.

This is completely unacceptable! Never step on anyone else to feel better. Remember, there is enough purpose for everyone. What goes around comes around and around, and around... Because we are in this world, our emotions may not always line up with the will or Word of God. But we must completely erase emotions from our daily decision making process and go with what's right.

Guard Your Gates

In order to erase emotions from your daily activities, you must properly guard your gates. Your eyes, your ears, and what you speak from your mouth have an effect on your soul. Each day we are bombarded with images. Movies that perpetuate lustful and violent acts are what people most often mention. These, while bad, are not the subtlest of culprits.

You also have advertisements that shape our concepts of beauty, celebrity gossip shows that make us covetous, and love stories that convince us that we can't live without the constant love and attention of a man or woman.

Lies, lies, all lies. First of all, who's to say that a person's baggy eyes or belly fat is unattractive? Who decided this? Who decided that certain features are attractive: a certain head size, hair texture, etc.? Who cares? We are all here for our holy directive. As I look around in public places and at all the people that I know, all I see is oh, that's Sister Hart or this is William. We usually don't see the same imperfections that people see in themselves. I don't even notice these "so called flaws" in other people until they themselves point them out.

However, I still have this need to fix my imperfections. And there is nothing wrong with wanting to fix them. But balance is needed in this. You can keep yourself clean, wear a fragrance, and take care of yourself by working out, but learn to like what you see. This goes to me first. Yeah, go ahead and try to achieve that certain "look" any way you can if it makes you feel better. If progress is a little too slow, just enjoy the process and be grateful for the results you have so far. In order to do that, guard your gates from those things that make you feel inferior.

While in your 3-bedroom home or studio apartment you saw the newest NBA draft pick's new house. Wow! It has marble floors and countertops, and 20 rooms. Stop watching these shows and go for a walk! Or better yet, go to a friend's and offer to clean their big house. You'll change your tune when you're worn out from cleaning five toilets!

I prefer scientific and psychological thrillers to love stories. Love stories depict a concept of love that is unrealistic and normally burns out after two years. No real couple is always sweetie sweetie and in each other's faces 24/7.

Half the time, you and your spouse's moods don't even match. He may be sweetie sweetie one day, while you are hyper-focused on a task and the same may be for him when you are all lovey-dovey. It is this fairytale depiction of love that has caused the divorce rate to increase so rapidly even among Christians! So guard your gates by putting in more biblical "screen time" than that spent looking at someone else's success or "perfect relationship" on social media.

Summary

Expect nothing and enjoy everything. Enjoy breathing. Enjoy the fact that you can get up and walk if you want to. Enjoy the sun; enjoy the weather, enjoy freedom. Find something positive in all you do and blow those things up to Godly proportions. "Lord, I thank you… I took a step, and another, and another… thank you Jesus!" Because of your gratefulness, if it's too hot outside, God may send a cool breeze to show you His approval. HEY YOU…GET A LIFE! LIVE A LIFE THAT IS PLEASING TO THE LORD!!!

About the Author

Meandria C. Tart-Baskin came up with The Handbook for the Easily Offended after prayer. Enduring a life of bullying, feelings of social isolation, and feelings of inadequacy, she sought Christ at a young age. It was her relationship with God that allowed her to do well academically and attend and complete college.

After life didn't yield what she

expected, she felt some of her old feelings resurface. The job market seemed to tell her that she was worthless and unremarkable. She continued in the Lord, but couldn't seem to shake the feelings of inadequacy within. During a layoff period, God gave her this book. What started off as a 30 page rant, became "Hey, You…Get a Life: The Handbook for the Easily Offended." Because she was so encouraged by it and felt changed, it became her goal to share this philosophy with others.

She has now settled into her role as an encourager. She seeks to encourage and inspire others to live a more abundant life in Christ, focusing on Him first and foremost.

She is heeding the warning in her white throne dream. She places her self-worth not in her accomplishments, nor in her interpersonal relationships but only in the hands of God.

Upcoming Publications

*Raising Heroes: Childrearing
from a Child's Perspective*

No More Blood

Illustrations

Ioahnna Stells
Inside Cover Art

Charles R. Tart., Jr.
Motherly Love
Your Cheating Heart

Tracy Isley
To BFF or Not to BFF
Compiled and Modified

Remaining Chapter Illustrations
Secured from Pexels.com
and modified

*****

Photographs

Dedication & *About the Author*
Courtesy of Meandria Tart-Baskin